GEO

HORSES SET II

PRZEWALSKI'S HORSES

Kristin Van Cleaf
ABDO Publishing Company

visit us at
www.abdopub.com

Published by ABDO Publishing Company, 4940 Viking Drive, Edina, Minnesota 55435.
Copyright © 2006 by Abdo Consulting Group, Inc. International copyrights reserved in all
countries. No part of this book may be reproduced in any form without written permission from
the publisher. The Checkerboard Library™ is a trademark and logo of ABDO Publishing
Company.

Printed in the United States.

Cover Photo: Corbis
Interior Photos: A.M. Groenveld / Foundation for the Preservation and Protection of the
    Przewalski Horse pp. 11, 13, 21; Animals Animals p. 7; Corbis pp. 14, 15, 19; Foundation for
    the Preservation and Protection of the Przewalski Horse p. 5; Peter Arnold p. 17; Visuals
    Unlimited p. 9

Series Coordinator: Heidi M. Dahmes
Editors: Heidi M. Dahmes, Stephanie Hedlund
Art Direction: Neil Klinepier

Library of Congress Cataloging-in-Publication Data

Van Cleaf, Kristin, 1976-
    Przewalski's horses / Kristin Van Cleaf.
        p. cm. -- (Horses. Set II)
    Includes bibliographical references.
    ISBN 1-59679-317-1
    1. Przewalski's horse--Juvenile literature. I. Title.

SF363.V36 2006
599.665'5--dc22
                                                                    2005045275

CONTENTS

WHERE PRZEWALSKI'S HORSES CAME FROM

Horses are an old species of mammal. Experts think they first appeared about 55 million years ago as a tiny animal called eohippus. Over time, horses grew and changed.

At first, humans hunted horses for their meat. But eventually, they began taming the animals. Horses were useful in farming, for riding, and even in war.

As humans began farming more, the land available for wild horses shrank. The horses were being hunted off. In the 1800s, it appeared that the only wild horses were in Poland and Russia.

But, people weren't sure whether there were any truly wild horses left in the world. The herds might have just been made of **domestic** horses that had escaped **captivity**. But, the Przewalski's (pshuh-VAHL-skeez) horse was about to be discovered.

The Przewalski's horse is the only true wild horse in the world.

In the 1880s, Nikolay Przhevalsky reported finding herds of wild horses near the Gobi Desert in Asia. The local hunters gave him a skull and skin to take back as proof. It was believed that Przhevalsky had discovered these horses. That is how the Przewalski's horse received its name.

It was later realized that Przhevalsky was not the first person to observe these horses. Two separate travelers had journeyed through Asia much earlier than Przhevalsky. Each of them recorded in their journals that they had seen wild horses.

After Przhevalsky's announcement, word spread that wild horses still existed. Rare animal collectors around the world soon wanted to capture the horses for their own. So, expeditions set out to catch the Przewalski's horses.

Capturing the shy horses was difficult. Full-grown horses were impossible to catch. But, some of the expeditions succeeded in capturing foals.

Keeping the horses alive was a problem, but some of the horses survived. People discovered the wild animals could not be tamed. Still, they became prized objects for nobles and popular zoo attractions.

The first two Przewalski's foals were caught in 1898. Their captors had planned to rear them on sheep's milk. The horses died shortly after they were caught.

What Makes Przewalski's Horses Special

When Przewalski's horses were being captured, they were also being hunted. The animals were slowly killed off. Shortly after **World War II**, it appeared Przewalski's horses only existed in zoos.

But life was not easy in the zoos. The formerly wild horses did not have enough space. Sometimes, there wasn't enough grass. People also discovered that the horses were **aggressive** in **captivity**. They could not be handled or trained for riding.

In addition, the zoos didn't trade the horses enough. So, the animals were forced to mate with their relatives. This made it more likely that foals would have diseases or defects.

By 1945, only three stallions and nine mares existed in zoos worldwide.

Due to these problems, a **captive** Przewalski's life span was short. The number of **pregnant** mares also decreased. And, newborn foals did not always survive. Something needed to be done to save these last wild horses from extinction.

People soon saw that Przewalski's horses needed to return to the wild to survive. In 1977, three people in Rotterdam, Netherlands, created the Foundation for the Preservation and Protection of the Przewalski Horse (FPPPH). At that time, only about 300 Przewalski's were left.

The foundation created a plan to return the animals to the wild. It started by giving zoos advice on how to **breed** Przewalski's horses. The foundation hoped to lessen inbreeding. This would create stronger, healthier offspring.

The group knew Przewalski's had to relearn how to find food and care for themselves. So, it also began buying healthy Przewalski's from zoos. The horses were moved to land set aside by the foundation.

In 1988, the foundation found a reserve in the **steppes** of Mongolia. The area is called Hustain Nuruu and is very similar to the Przewalski's original homeland. It became Hustai National Park, protecting both the land and the horses from outside influence.

The Przewalski's horse is the national symbol of Mongolia. In Mongolia, these horses are called takhi.

WHERE PRZEWALSKI'S HORSES LIVE

In 1990, the FPPPH teamed up with the Mongolian Association for Conservation of Nature and Environment. The two groups worked together to plan for the return of the Przewalski's horse to the wild.

In June 1992, 16 Przewalski's horses were sent to Mongolia. Two more groups eventually joined them. They were kept in a mountain **steppe** reserve.

At first, the horses lived in a special area of the reserve. There, they could adjust to the new climate, plants, and other animals. This also allowed the individual horses to become used to each other and form family groups. Eventually, the Przewalski's were released into the reserve's wild areas.

Many steppe regions in the world have been lost. With the preservation of the Przewalski's horse, steppes are also being saved.

WHAT PRZEWALSKI'S HORSES LOOK LIKE

A Przewalski's horse is sturdy and compact. Horses are measured in four-inch (10-cm) units called hands. The Przewalski's horse stands 12 to 14 hands high.

The Przewalski's neck is strong and short. The head is heavy, with a long face. The eyes are dark and sit close to the ears.

This horse's mane and tail are dark. The mane hairs are stiff, so they stand upright. The hair

A Przewalski's sheds its mane every summer. So, its mane is short, and there is no forelock.

stops between the ears, so there is no **forelock**. The tail hairs are short at the top of the tail. Lower down, they grow longer.

The Przewalski's coat is light brown, sandy, or reddish bay. Around the eyes, **muzzle**, and on the stomach, the coat is cream colored. A dark stripe runs down its back. Its lower legs are dark, or often have stripes similar to those of a zebra.

A Przewalski's horse is shy, but highly alert. It has a shrill voice, as well as excellent senses of hearing and smell. These **traits** all serve to protect it from danger.

Przewalski's horses help each other keep their skin in good condition. The horses cannot reach their own backs, so they nibble each other's skin. This is called mutual grooming.

FEEDING

Przewalski's horses live in groups. The two types are family and bachelor. A family group has a stallion and three or four mares with their foals and some yearlings. In a bachelor group, an elder stallion leads the younger stallions.

Each group has a home area. An area has enough food, water, and shelter for the group. Sometimes they need to **migrate** to have enough resources. Occasionally, groups will share resources.

In summer early mornings and evenings, a group will graze in meadows and drink from small streams. In the warmest part of the day and at night they will rest. One horse will keep watch for danger at night.

The Przewalski's horse is an herbivore. This means it does not eat meat. It will feed on grass, other plants, and fruit. Occasionally, it will even eat tree bark, leaves, and buds.

A mature male horse is called a stallion.
The female is known as a mare.

How Przewalski's Horses Grow

A Przewalski's mare starts having foals when she is about three years old. She is **pregnant** for about 11 to 12 months. In Mongolia, the birth season is around the end of May, June, and July.

An hour after birth, the foal will be able to stand and even walk. It will drink its mother's milk. Within a few weeks, it will start to eat grass. But, the foal is not **weaned** until it is 8 to 13 months old. Foals have a better chance of survival now that they have returned to the wild.

A Przewalski's stallion starts looking for mating partners when he is about five years old. His instinct will be to create a group of mares. Often, he will wander until he finds another group with its own leader.

At this point, the young stallion may fight the current leader. The fight may last days, or sometimes weeks. If the young stallion is victorious, the mares must adjust to the new leader. Sometimes, the mares will leave the group and find another.

There is not much fighting among family members. Fighting wastes energy and can leave wounds. Families work together in order to survive.

Przewalski's Horses Today

So far, the program to return Przewalski's horses to the wild has been successful. There are now about 150 of these horses in the wild. However, more work still needs to be done.

The FPPPH hopes to expand the Hustai National Park population to at least 500 animals. This will ensure that they have a strong group that can survive diseases and **predators**.

Part of the plan includes protecting the land in Hustai National Park. The foundation continues to help the local people to care for their land and animals.

Today, the Przewalski's horse is still an **endangered** species. Only about 1,450 exist in zoos, private parks, and in the wild. But, projects such as the reintroduction plan have created hope for the future.

Today, Przewalski's horses roam free among the forest and steppe regions in Hustai National Park.

GLOSSARY

aggressive - displaying hostility.

breed - a group of animals sharing the same appearance and characteristics. A breeder is a person who raises animals. Raising animals is often called breeding them.

captivity - the state of being captured and held against one's will.

domestic - animals that are tame.

endangered - in danger of becoming extinct.

forelock - a tuft of hair growing above the forehead.

migrate - to move from one place to another, often to find food.

muzzle - an animal's nose and jaws.

predator - an animal that kills and eats other animals.

pregnant - having one or more babies growing within the body.

steppe - any large, flat plain without trees.

trait - a quality that distinguishes one person or group from another.

wean - to accustom an animal to eat food other than its mother's milk.

World War II - from 1939 to 1945, fought in Europe, Asia, and Africa. Great Britain, France, the United States, the Soviet Union, and their allies were on one side. Germany, Italy, Japan, and their allies were on the other side.

WEB SITES

To learn more about Przewalski's horses, visit ABDO Publishing Company on the World Wide Web at **www.abdopub.com**. Web sites about these horses are featured on our Book Links page. These links are routinely monitored and updated to provide the most current information available.

INDEX